Girls'

GOLF

by Maryann Hudson

GIRLS'

SportsZone

Published by ABDO Publishing Company, PO Box 398166, Minneapolis, MN 55439. Copyright © 2014 by Abdo Consulting Group, Inc. International copyrights reserved in all countries. No part of this book may be reproduced in any form without written permission from the publisher. SportsZone™ is a trademark and logo of ABDO Publishing Company.

Printed in the United States of America,
North Mankato, Minnesota

052013
092013

 THIS BOOK CONTAINS AT LEAST 10% RECYCLED MATERIALS.

Editor: Chrös McDougall
Series Designer: Marie Tupy

Photo Credits: Steve Cukrov/Shutterstock Images, cover, 1; Mark Avery/AP Images, 5; Chris Carlson/ AP Images, 7, 9; Charles Baus/Icon SMI, 10; Kyodo News/AP Images, 13, 15; Ross D. Franklin/AP Images, 18; The Canadian Press, Darryl Dyck/AP Images, 21, 23, 26; Rodrigo Pena/AP Images, 25; Steve Helber/AP Images, 29; AP Images, 32; Jon Super/AP Images, 34; Mike Fiala/AP Images, 37, 38; Seth Perlman/AP Images, 40; Wong Maye-E/AP Images, 42; Shutterstock Images, 44

Library of Congress Control Number: 2013932513

Cataloging-in-Publication Data

Hudson, Maryann.
 Girls' golf / Maryann Hudson.
  p. cm. -- (Girls' sportszone)
 ISBN 978-1-61783-985-6 (lib. bdg.)
 Includes bibliographical references and index.
 1. Golf for girls--Juvenile literature. I. Title.
 796.352--dc23

                                                    2013932513

GIRLS' SportsZone

1 **Driving with Brittany Lincicome** 4

2 **The Mental Game with Stacy Lewis** 12

3 **Putting with Lydia Ko** 20

4 **The Short Game:**
Michelle Wie vs. Yani Tseng 28

5 **The Total Game with Annika Sorenstam** 36

Hole Diagram   44

Glossary   45

For More Information   46

Index   48

About the Author   48

1

Driving with Brittany Lincicome

Brittany Lincicome, Cristie Kerr, and Kristy McPherson walked to the 18th tee at the 2009 Kraft Nabisco Championship at Mission Hills Golf Course in Rancho Mirage, California. It was the final round of the major tournament. Kerr and McPherson had taken turns leading the tournament the entire round. Now, with one hole to play, McPherson held a 1-stroke lead. Lincicome and Kerr were one stroke back.

The 18th hole was a 485-yard (443 m), par-5, with water in front of the green. But driving the ball is Lincicome's strength. She blasted her drive 275 yards (251 m) to the middle of the fairway. Now she had a choice. She could lay up in front of the water or go for the green. With a similar choice, McPherson decided to lay up. Lincicome decided to go for it.

Brittany Lincicome tees off on the 16th hole during the 2009 Kraft Nabisco Championship.

"BAM-BAM"

Kristy McPherson calls Brittany Lincicome "Bam-Bam" because she hits the ball so far. Lincicome has the statistics to back up that nickname. She led the 2012 Ladies Professional Golf Association (LPGA) in driving distance with an average drive of 276.083 yards (252.450 m). In each of her seven years on the tour through 2012, Lincicome finished the season ranked in the top three in driving distance. In her rookie season of 2005, she finished first. Her average drive that year was 270.300 yards (247.162 m).

Throughout the round, Lincicome had stayed within three strokes of the lead, but there was nothing soothing to her about that. She was admittedly a nervous wreck. She spent the entire day trying to calm down. She sang country songs and thought about fishing and being with her dog, Bunker. But at the turn, she told her good friend McPherson she thought she was going to have a heart attack.

"My heart is beating out of my chest," Lincicome said.

Lincicome grew up in Saint Petersburg, Florida. She was always playing golf with her father and brothers, so she wanted to hit the ball far to keep up with them. By 2009 she was one of the most powerful women's golfers. Now she had an opportunity to prove it.

It was 210 yards (192 m) to the pin. Lincicome grabbed a hybrid club. Her hands were shaking. Her heart was racing.

"I'm trying to calm myself down by breathing or singing or whatever I can possibly do, and right when I hit it, it came off on the club face exactly where we wanted to hit it and took the slope like I wanted it to and came really close, thank God," Lincicome said.

Brittany Lincicome watches her second shot on the 18th hole at the 2009 Kraft Nabisco Championship as Kristy McPherson walks by.

GRIPS FOR SUCCESS

Like many young golfers, Brittany Lincicome started out using a two-handed grip. This grip, which is similar to a baseball grip, gives the golfer more power. With a baseball grip, the golfer puts both hands on the grip, one above the other, as a bat would be held. Lincicome later switched to an overlapping grip for better accuracy. The overlapping grip and the interlock grip are common for golfers who have established some power. For right-handers, the pinky finger sits comfortably between the two knuckles of the left fore and middle fingers with an overlap grip. With an interlock grip, the pinky finger of the right hand hooks around the forefinger of the left hand. This forms a strong physical connection and is also sometimes used by golfers with small hands to get a better grip.

The ball flew over the water and landed on the upper part of the two-tiered green. Then it rolled down the slope to stop four feet (1.2 m) from the hole. "If I had to make anything farther than that . . . my hands were shaking so bad, I was almost crying," she said.

Kerr made an 18-foot (5.5 m) birdie putt from the fringe to tie McPherson, who made par. But it was soon over for the two players who had led all day. Lincicome rolled the 4-foot (1.2 m) putt in for an eagle to win the major by a single stroke. She finished the round at a 3-under-par 69 and 9-under for the tournament.

Then she jumped into Poppy's Pond with her father and caddie, a tradition for the winner of the Kraft Nabisco Championship.

Swinging with Power

The drive is one of the most important and nerve-racking shots in golf.
No matter what happens on a hole, there's another tee shot lurking ahead.
Until the final hole, there's no escape. Hitting a good drive means a greater
opportunity to score low on a hole. If it's a short hole, commonly a par-3,
a good drive lands on or close to the green. That increases the chances for
a birdie or par. If it's a long hole, commonly a par-4 or par-5, a good drive
stops in the fairway in a good position for the second shot. Crushing the
ball off the tee is great, but not if it disappears off the fairway.

When she addresses the ball, Lincicome sets up with her right shoulder
lower than her left, tilted away from the ball. This allows her to wind up

Brittany Lincicome, *center*, jumps in the pond with her caddie, *left*, and
her dad after winning the 2009 Kraft Nabisco Championship.

9

with a big turn in her backswing and helps to hit the ball on the upswing as she comes down. It also helps create a big throwing motion on the downswing. Lincicome makes a huge extension off the ball. However, her speed comes from clubhead lag—she slings the clubhead at the last second for a burst of speed. Her hips also start turning forward before her shoulders finish turning back.

The faster the clubhead speed, the farther the ball will travel. Clubhead speed is measured in miles per hour. It indicates how fast the club travels when it makes impact with the ball.

Brittany Lincicome follows through on a shot during the final round of the 2009 Kraft Nabisco Championship.

Quick Tip: Swinging Free

A main component of a powerful drive is to be relaxed and swing freely. That's easier said than done, especially on the first tee with people watching and waiting. There are ways to get better though. Without using a golf ball, try swinging a golf club the same way a baseball bat is swung, on a horizontal plane. In a baseball swing, the arms and hands swing more relaxed and natural. This drill helps to learn how to control the club by swinging freely. It also helps to feel the rotation of the forearms and club, all of which creates more clubhead speed. The world's top-ranked amateur in 2012, Lydia Ko, used this exercise before teeing off at the Canadian Open that year. She went on to win. In her case, it helped to get her swing less steep and back on plane.

The tighter the body is coiled at the top of the backswing, the faster the club will travel forward. It's similar to the principle of shooting a rubber band. The tighter the band, the farther it flies. Clubhead speed is also increased when the body is relaxed, so the club swings smoother and faster. The key is to swing faster but not harder.

"I have grown up playing men so I never thought of it as hitting it that far," Lincicome said. "It just seemed normal to me, but I do get a thrill out of it. I never hold back because I love to gamble and push the envelope. Working out and technology also have a lot to do with my hitting it far."

2

The Mental Game
with Stacy Lewis

Stacy Lewis was so far off the lead starting the final round of the
2012 Mizuno Classic in Japan that no one gave her a thought. No
one, that is, except for her.

Lewis had hope. But she also had nerves, and she knew she would have
to control the pressure and stay mentally tough to make a charge. She was
in a tight race for the LPGA Player of the Year Award. No American-born
golfer had won the award in 18 years, and Lewis wanted it.

Overall, Lewis was having a strong season. By midsummer, she was
ranked second in the world. But South Korean Inbee Park was challenging
Lewis for the award. Mentally, Lewis was rattled. She started thinking
too hard.

Stacy Lewis watches her shot during the final round of the 2012
Mizuno Classic in Japan.

"I was thinking, this putt, this shot, is going to mean I win Player of the Year," Lewis said, "and when you're thinking like that, it's hard to free yourself up and hit shots. It was probably more pressure than I've ever felt. I didn't know what I was doing."

Lewis, 27, knew she needed to settle her mind down before this tournament. So she talked with Beth Daniel. In 1994 Daniel was the last American to win the Player of the Year Award. Daniel counseled Lewis on the mental game. Daniel reminded Lewis how great she had been playing and told her to enjoy herself no matter what happens.

That morning at the Mizuno, Lewis made her move. She made seven birdies to move within one stroke of South Korea's Bo-Mee Lee with four holes left to play. Then, on the 16th hole, she hit trouble. Her second shot landed in a fairway bunker. But Lewis handled the pressure. She hit out of the bunker to 25 feet (7.6 m) from the hole. Then she sank the putt. Lewis made a 12-footer (3.7 m) on the 17th hole. She made another 25-footer (7.6 m) on the final hole to finish with three consecutive birdies. She finished with a one-stroke victory.

"I pulled a lot off [Beth Daniel] on how to handle my emotions and the pressure," Lewis said. "She always told me, 'You just have to be yourself, you're not Paula [Creamer] or Natalie [Gulbis], you're Stacy.'"

Stacy Lewis holds the trophy after winning the 2012 Mizuno Classic in Japan.

A LONG ROAD TO STARDOM

Working through tough situations is nothing new to Lewis. She wore a back brace for seven and a half years from age 11. The brace was needed to correct a condition called scoliosis, which caused a curvature in her spine. It embarrassed her. The only time she could remove the brace was when she played golf or went swimming. When Lewis was 18, she had back surgery. During a four-hour operation, doctors removed part of a rib and put in a steel rod with five screws into five vertebrae. "That was the time that, I mean, I thought I would never play golf again," Lewis said. "Now 10 years later I'm here winning Player of the Year. That's crazy."

Lewis ended the season with 221 points to win the Player of the Year Award. Park was 53 points back in second place. For the season, Lewis won four tournaments and had 16 top-ten finishes.

"To play that well when the pressure is on, that's the ultimate," Lewis said of the Mizuno. "It sealed everything and put an exclamation point on the year."

No Head Games

Playing a good round of golf is determined not only by physical skill but by how the mind handles the game. Golf is naturally a slow game. Golfers have to walk a long way between shots and wait for their partners to take their shots. There's too much time to think on the golf course. Finding ways to shake off bad shots and keep a calm frame of mind is important. Mind skills help. With visualization, a golfer can see the shot ahead of time—where the ball will fly and how it will land. This can subconsciously tell the muscles what to do.

In 2011, Lewis finished second to Yani Tseng for the Player of the Year Award. Tseng, who is from Taiwan, handles the mental game by trying not to think too much when she's on the course.

"When I'm out there, I don't think about anything," she said. "I just grip it and rip it. I don't like to worry about technique."

Tseng writes herself notes to remember to smile between shots and to walk the course with confidence. Gary Gilchrist is Tseng's coach. He says Tseng didn't have the mental toughness when she started on tour. She was a bundle of nerves.

"Her post-shot routine was bad; she used to get down on herself very quickly," he said. Through the years, he has given Tseng the following advice:

LEXI THOMPSON: RELAX

Scott Thompson recalls a time when his daughter, golfer Lexi Thompson, had a sour attitude when she wasn't hitting well during a practice round in an American Junior Golf Association event. He pulled her out of the tournament. "I've always been a fiery, competitive person," she said. "I've learned now you need to have fun when you play and be more relaxed. I think back then . . . I was really too serious. But I am still focused on playing really well."

Think positive thoughts between shots and carry yourself with good posture.

Focus on what you do well and don't put more pressure on yourself.

Stay patient and on the same track.

Lewis said she learned from watching Tseng on the course.

"She [Tseng] didn't play great all the time, but she played great when she had to," Lewis said. "That's what great players do, when you have to

Stacy Lewis sinks a putt for birdie during the 2013 Founders Cup in Phoenix, Arizona.

Quick Tip: Take Your Mind Away

Find ways to keep your mind from overthinking the next shot, or the last bad shot, by doing puzzles while waiting to hit. Brittany Lincicome has worked on Sudoku puzzles and played hangman games during her rounds. One Sudoku puzzle kept her stumped for weeks. Lincicome said, "So if you're on a par-3 or you have like a long wait, it's just something to kind of take my mind off of playing golf." Lincicome also loves to fish. She named her fishing boat "Taking Relief."

make a good putt, or shoot a good score, or get up and down, they do it at the right time. And that's the biggest difference."

Lewis now says she loves the pressure that comes with winning.

"Feeling those nerves down the stretch, that's what I play for," Lewis said. "To see how different people handle it, how you handle it. Every situation is different. . . . I live for it."

chapter 3

Putting with Lydia Ko

Lydia Ko made the turn tied for the lead in the final round of the 2012 Canadian Women's Open. Then the teenager from New Zealand raced through the remaining nine holes like she was being timed. Ko snacked on cherry tomatoes to keep up her energy. She birdied the 10th, 11th, 12th, and 13th holes. When she missed her short putt for birdie on the 14th, she walked off the green giggling with her caddie. Then, on her way to the 15th tee, she even stopped to autograph a fan's hat.

Golf is supposed to be fun, right?

At 15 years, 4 months, and 2 days old, Ko had five birdies in a stretch of six holes on the back nine. That helped her become the youngest

Lydia Ko was all smiles as she waited to tee off on the 18th hole in the third round at the 2012 Canadian Women's Open.

KO'S TROPHY CASE

Lydia Ko was five when her aunt gave her a 7-iron and a putter. Her family had recently moved from South Korea to New Zealand. Ko started taking lessons from coach Guy Wilson. At age seven, she competed in the New Zealand Women's Amateur. She won that event seven years later. At 12, she tied for seventh in a Ladies European Tour event. At 14, she won the New South Wales Open to become the youngest winner on the Australian LPGA Tour.

In 2012, Ko was the low amateur at the US Women's Open. That meant she had the best score of any amateur in the tournament. However, that event was a tune-up. In mid-August, Ko won the US Women's Amateur Championship. Two weeks later, she became the youngest winner of an LPGA event when she won the Canadian Women's Open, beating an impressive field of professionals. At 15 years, 4 months, and 2 days, Ko was more than a year younger than the previous youngest winner.

tournament winner in LPGA history. She also became the first amateur in 43 years to win an LPGA event, since JoAnne Carner in 1969. Ko beat South Korean Inbee Park by three strokes.

"It's great to win, and the last few holes it got a bit nerve-racking, but Stacy Lewis, after my birdie on 15, she said, you know, you can do it," Ko said.

Ko's perfect tempo in her stroke had putts dropping like they were being pulled to the center of the earth. She smiled widely throughout this run. After making her final birdie on the 15th hole, Ko gave high fives to fans as she walked to the 16th tee.

"I tried to smile the whole round, and I guess it worked," Ko said. "I try to smile even after a bogey. It may seem a little crazy, smiling and laughing after a mistake, but it was great."

Ko said she found new confidence in her putting during the 2012 US Women's Amateur Championship. In Ko's semifinal match, Ariya Jutanugarn of Thailand outdrove her by about 40 yards (37 m) on most

Lydia Ko putts during the third round of the 2012 Canadian Women's Open.

of the holes. But Ko won the match with a poised short game that included just 23 putts. She called it the best putting day she ever had.

"My putting is really not the strong point of my game . . . I wasn't having a good day with my long game, but my putting just saved me," Ko said. "That's why I was able to win most of my matches. From there, I kind of realized that you don't need to have the best day in your long game to shoot low scores. It's mostly about putting. That's why people say drives are all for show and putting is for money. . . . It gave me a lot of confidence."

Putting It In

Golfers generally use their putters more than any other club in a round of golf. Every hole starts with a drive and almost every hole ends with a putt. However, golfers use different clubs on the drive depending on the hole. Once the ball is on the green, golfers carry just one putter.

There are a few basic qualities that make up good putting. They are proper alignment for aiming, a smooth stroke with good tempo, a soft grip, and distance control. From and within those skills, a golfer develops the all-important feel and touch needed to become a good putter.

There are many different ways to perform those skills. For example, there are different types of putting grips and different ways to aim. But what's important is for each golfer to discover what works best for her. The confidence that carries over from making a putt is invaluable on the next tee.

Lydia Ko and her caddie react as her putt rolls toward the cup during the 2013 Kraft Nabisco Championship.

Ko uses a different putting grip than most golfers. Her grip is called "lead-hand low." Another name for it is "cross-handed." Normally, a right-handed golfer holds the putter with the left hand on top and the right hand below. Ko, who is right-handed, putts with her right hand on top and her left hand below.

There are advantages to the lead-hand-low grip. It helps keep the right hand from taking over at impact. It eliminates any excess movement in the wrist and hands. It eliminates forearm rotation. It also encourages the shoulders to be square to the line at address and promotes a square putter face through impact.

Strong putting helped Lydia Ko win the 2012 Canadian Women's Open.

Quick Tip: The Inner Putt

Both short and long putts require concentration, practice, and feel. Here's a short-putting exercise to help get on track. Start putting about a foot (0.3 m) from the hole. Watch and hear the ball drop into the hole. Do this a few times, and then slowly work back and hit some more.

Some golfers use the left-hand low grip only on shorter putts. They don't believe this grip gives them the feel required to make a long or breaking putt.

As with all things in golf, the key to good putting is to stay relaxed, focused, and composed. Guy Wilson is Ko's coach. He said composure comes naturally with Ko.

"She just tends to sort of phase most things out and put herself in her own little environment and hit shot after shot," Wilson said.

Ko also works with a mental skills coach named David Niethe.

"She [Ko] has this ability to stay in the present, and she does that so effectively," said Niethe, who has worked with Ko for five years. Niethe said Ko's humble confidence and focus is remarkable.

"She will have an intense focus on a shot at hand then she'll just have a whole lot of fun."

4

The Short Game: Michelle Wie vs. Yani Tseng

Michelle Wie was 14. Yani Tseng was 15. Wie, from Hawaii, was the defending champion of the US Women's Amateur Public Links Championship. She had won in 2003 when she was 13. That made her the youngest golfer to win what is considered an adult tournament.

Now, a year later, she was defending her title against Tseng, a great young golfer from Taiwan. They matched up at the Golden Horseshoe Golf Club in Williamsburg, Virginia.

Both golfers were known for crushing their drives off the tee. However, this 2004 match-play championship was decided not with their long games but with their short games.

Michelle Wie chips up to the 15th green during the 2004 US Women's Amateur Public Links Championship.

Tseng had trailed Wie for most of the day but tied her on the 32nd hole. The match was still tied as they entered the final hole. It was a 466-yard (426 m) par-5 that sloped uphill to a green surrounded by a couple of bunkers. Wie hit her second shot into a bunker. Tseng had an iron in her hand to make her second shot. However, she changed her mind and switched to a wood. She decided to go for the green.

Most golfers do their best to stay clear of bunkers, but not Tseng. If she couldn't hit over it, she was fine hitting into it.

"I saw Michelle put it in the bunker," Tseng said. "Even though the distance [to the green was] 225 [feet (68.6 m)], but even if I didn't carry it, I'm comfortable with the sand. So that's why I did it, [hitting it] right into the bunker."

PRETEND IT'S PRACTICE

On the par-3, 27th hole of the 2012 US Women's Amateur Championship final, Lydia Ko's ball landed in a greenside bunker. She faced a difficult 20-yard (18.2 m) shot to the hole. Her ball was on a downhill lie on damp sand. She had to hit over the bunker's high lip. There was just 12 feet (3.7 m) of green. Ko's mom, Tina, told her daughter, "Try that flop bunker shot that you practice for fun. Be aggressive. Pretend it's a practice shot." Ko's ball shot from a plume of sand. It rolled over the edge of the hole and stopped three feet (0.9 m) from the hole. She made par and kept her lead of 4-up with nine holes to play against American Jaye Marie Green, whom Ko later defeated for the title.

Wie's ball was in the left bunker about 30 yards (27 m) from the hole. She hit out of the sand too softly and left a 24-foot (7.3 m) uphill putt for birdie. Tseng was in the front bunker. She blasted out to 12 feet (3.7 m) from the cup.

Wie's putt tailed off short. She slumped over for several moments. Tseng paced back and forth before putting. Her ball hit the cup dead center for a birdie. She had won the tournament 1-up.

Tseng went for the green on her second shot because she knew if she landed in the sand she could get out.

Her confidence in her short game determined her strategy to go for the green. The year before, in the same tournament, it was Wie's sand shot that helped her win. Wie had trailed Virada Nirapathpongporn all day. She tied the match on the 24th hole with a birdie after she flew a sand shot over a water hazard and onto the green. It was risky, but it worked.

TROPHY CASE

Yani Tseng and Michelle Wie were both teen sensations. Tseng won 15 international tournaments and four US events before she turned professional in 2007 at age 18. She kept going strong as a pro. Tseng's five major championships before age 22 made her the youngest to reach that milestone. Wie set many local, state, and national records as an amateur. In 2004 she shot the lowest round (68) ever recorded by a woman in a Professional Golfers' Association Tour (men's) event. She turned pro at age 15 in 2005. For several years, she divided her time between golf and attending Stanford University. She graduated in 2012.

Sizing Up a Short Game

Scoring in golf is about the short game. And the short game is about distance control. For most golfers, the short game is played within 100 yards (91.4 m) of the green with the intention of getting the ball close to the cup. This can be a stressful time. It's an area where a dozen different situations can—and do—occur. Just when the ball is getting closer to the hole, there's water, or rough, or the dreaded greenside bunker.

Yani Tseng chips on her way to a second-place finish at a 2008 tournament in China.

There are special shots and special clubs made just for the short game. The basic shots are pitch, chip, bunker, and flop. The clubs generally used are irons and wedges. Wedges have lofts and soles that help get the ball up and over hazards and out of sand and thick grass.

The pitch shot is generally hit within 30 yards (27.4 m) from the green, though it can be hit from farther away. The shot is rightly named, because it's used to get the ball up in the air with limited roll on the green. Golfers pitch when there are obstacles to hit over or to hit out of thick grass.

The length of the swing and the club determines the distance of the shot. Wedge clubs are used for pitching because of their loft. The degree of loft determines how high the shot will go. The degree increases from the pitching wedge to the gap, sand, and lob wedge. The higher the loft, the less distance the ball will travel and the less it will roll when it lands.

Chip shots are used from the fringe or just off the green in short grass to get the ball on the green and rolling like a putt. They should have about one-third airtime and two-thirds roll. Golfers also use this shot to chip out of a hard-sand bunker if there is no lip on the edge. Usually less lofted clubs, such as a 7, 8, or 9 iron, are used.

From bunkers, there are many variables, but a sand wedge is usually used for bunker shots. If the hole is really close, golfers often use a higher loft wedge to go a shorter distance with less roll. Sand shots require a full

Michelle Wie chips out of the rough toward the green during the 2012 Women's British Open.

Quick Tip: Chip-Putt-Drop

Here's a shot that can help when the ball is close to the green but the lie won't allow for a smooth stroke with a putter. It's a chip-putt. Treat it like a putt. Read the green, then set up for a chip shot. Use a short iron such as a 7 or 8. Use the normal putting grip. The ball should be in the middle of the stance. Maintain good posture with more weight on the left foot. Choke down on the club so the iron feels about the same length as a putter. Use a putting stroke. The length of the swing determines the distance.

swing and high finish. A half-swing will only get the ball half out of the sand. The swing needs to hit the sand about two inches (5 cm) behind the ball. The sand explosion drives the ball out of the bunker.

The last type of short game shot is a flop shot. This is the shot Lydia Ko hit out of the bunker on the 27th hole of the US Amateur. It goes high and has little or no roll. It is used when close to the green to get over obstacles or to get out of bunkers when there is little green to work with. The shot is played with a lob wedge.

chapter 5

The Total Game with Annika Sorenstam

It was March 16, 2001. The gallery behind Annika Sorenstam emptied as she walked down the final stretch at Moon Valley Country Club in Phoenix, Arizona. As she passed each section, the applause grew. Fans left their places and scrambled to follow Sorenstam's every move. History was being made in the second round at the 2001 Standard Register PING tournament, and nobody in the gallery wanted to miss it.

The Swedish golfer and her caddie, Terry McNamara, stood on the fairway of the final hole and discussed her second shot. It was a par-4 hole. If Sorenstam made par, she would end with a score of 59 for the round. That would be the lowest in LPGA history.

Annika Sorenstam celebrates after she birdied a hole in the final round of the 2001 Standard Register PING tournament.

"I am so pumped, my heart rate, I think you could see the shirt moving," she said. "I was in-between clubs and there was a water hazard in the front. My caddie said to take one more club to get on the green. I said, 'Nope, I'm going for the flag.' I hit it straight at the flag for an eight- or nine-footer at the edge."

Sorenstam putted to within three feet (0.9 m) and then tapped in. The crowd went wild. Sorenstam jumped into the arms of her caddie. She was the first female to break a score of 60 in an official event.

"A tip I give a lot is the importance of staying focused on the shot and ignoring distractions," Sorenstam said. "I was definitely practicing what I

Annika Sorenstam lines up her putt on the 13th green during the 2001 Standard Register PING tournament.

preach during my final putt. It was the longest three-foot (0.9 m) putt I have ever faced, but I did my best to not think about the pressure."

Sorenstam's round was great from the beginning.

"I started the day and I was feeling good," said Sorenstam, who made eight consecutive birdies. "After five birdies I asked my caddie, 'How many birdies in a row have you seen?' And he said five or six. So I said, 'Let's keep going.' So I made eight birdies in a row and now I wasn't so comfortable any more. So I told my caddie Terry that I needed to make par on the 9th hole."

She parred the 9th hole. Then Sorenstam decided she wanted more birdies. ". . . and I rattled off another four," Sorenstam said. "It was amazing. The cup was as big as a bucket and whatever I did it went in. . . . I'm starting to think, 'This is not an ordinary day. What am I doing? What's happening?'"

A LEGEND IN THE GAME

Annika Sorenstam was born in 1970 in Stockholm, Sweden. During her 15-year pro golf career, she won 72 LPGA championships, including 10 majors. She won eight LPGA Player of the Year Awards. That is also a record. Her score of 59 earned her the nickname "Ms. 59." Sorenstam was the first and, through 2012, still the only female to cross the $20 million mark for LPGA career earnings. She was inducted into the World Golf Hall of Fame in 2003 and retired after the 2008 season. She started the Annika Academy in Orlando, Florida, one of her many businesses.

Sorenstam ended her round of 59 at 13-under par. She needed only 25 putts. She made 13 birdies and no bogeys. She missed only one fairway. She reached every green in regulation and her longest putt for par was 3.5 feet (1.1 m). Her score of 59 beat the previous LPGA low score of 61 shared by Karrie Webb and Se Ri Pak. Two days later, she won the tournament by two strokes at 27-under par.

Have a Plan

Sorenstam was known as an extremely focused player before retiring in 2008. With her coaches, including Pia Nilsson and Lynn Marriott, she made routines for her golf game. She believes her routines simplify the

Annika Sorenstam watches her drive off the tee during a 2007 tournament in Illinois.

game and will help a golfer become a smarter, more focused player.

The first step is establishing a pre-shot routine. Sorenstam said a good routine puts a golfer in a present state so she is less worried about the result and more focused on the shot at hand. It also establishes a positive mind-set for her swing.

DECIDE AND GO WITH IT

Make a club choice and stick with it. Annika Sorenstam said when it comes to picking the shot and club it's important not to overthink. "Consider the lie, the target, and any trouble in your way, but keep it simple," she wrote. "Once you make a decision, focus only on what you need to do—no second-guessing."

"Because you've performed the routine hundreds of times before, its familiarity will put you at ease," she said. "The swing follows naturally."

Sorenstam says her pre-shot routine takes just 24 seconds.

"I start by placing my hand on the bag—that is my cue to begin," she said. "Next, I grab the club I'm going to hit, stand a few feet behind the ball and visualize the shot I want to play. I take one practice swing to get loose and find my rhythm, and then walk to the ball, where I set my feet, relax my arms and look at the target one last time. I take just four or five seconds over the ball. This way, there's no time to overthink the shot. I just swing away."

Finally, Sorenstam says to only hit when ready. Sorenstam recalls a time when she didn't follow her pre-shot routine and the results weren't good. She was tied for the lead of a tournament on the 18th hole. The group in front of her took a long time to clear the green, and Sorenstam said she just stood on the fairway, leaning on her sand wedge.

"Big mistake," she said. "When my time came to hit, I chunked the shot into the water. I scored a double-bogey 7 and lost the tournament by one shot."

Annika Sorenstam chips the ball onto the green during a 2008 tournament in Singapore.

Quick Tip: The Think Box and the Play Box

Annika Sorenstam has an exercise to help organize her pre-shot routine. She divides the pre-shot area in two with an imaginary line or stick. Sorenstam calls the area behind her bag "The Think Box." This is where she thinks, sees the shot, and takes practice swings. Once she steps up to the ball to line up the club, she steps into the "Play Box." In the Play Box, there is no more thinking. No last-minute changes. No hesitating. Just hit the ball.

Continued Sorenstam, "I knew I should have put the wedge away while I waited. I never stand there with a club in my hand. My routine starts when I put my hand on my bag. Because I'd changed my routine, I wasn't in the right frame of mind to execute the shot. If you encounter a long delay, wait until it's your turn to hit before preparing for the shot. If the wait is longer than you anticipated, don't stand there holding a club; put it back. Turn your attention away from the green. If you have a tendency to get stiff, do some stretching exercises."

Hole Diagram

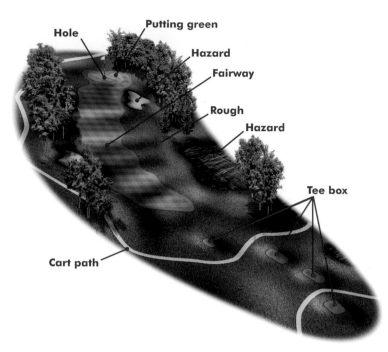

Hole • Putting green • Hazard • Fairway • Rough • Hazard • Tee box • Cart path

fairway

An area between the tee box and putting green in which the grass is cut short and even for easier approach shots.

hazards

Obstacles on the course. The most common hazards are sand bunkers and bodies of water.

putting green

The area surrounding the hole that has very short grass and a smooth surface for putting.

rough

Areas of long grass that surround the fairway and are more difficult to play from.

tee box

The area from which each hole begins. Golfers hit their first shot off a tee from this area. Holes usually have more than one tee box for golfers of various abilities.

amateur

Somebody who is not paid for playing golf.

bunker

A hazard on a golf course. Usually bunkers are shallow areas of sand.

chip

A short shot near the green, designed to spend a little time in the air and roll safely onto the green toward the cup.

lie

The place where a ball sits.

majors

The five most prestigious women's golf tournaments held each year. They are the Kraft Nabisco Championship, the LPGA Championship, the US Women's Open, the Women's British Open, and the Evian Masters.

match-play

A scoring format in which players or teams compete against each other on a hole-by-hole basis. The total number of strokes does not determine the winner. Instead, the number of holes won determines the winner.

par

The number of shots it should take an elite golfer to complete a course or a given hole.

pitch

A longer shot to the green made with a lofted club from several yards to about 100 yards (91 m) from the green. A pitch is used to get over an obstacle.

professional

A person who makes money by playing or teaching golf.

Selected Bibliography

Golf Magazine. *The Best Short Game Instruction Book Ever!* New York: Time Inc. Home Entertainment, 2009.

Penick, Harvey, with Bud Shrake. *Harvey Penick's Little Red Book*. New York: Simon & Schuster, 1992.

Werner, Doug. *Golfer's Start-Up: A Beginner's Guide to Golf*. San Diego: Tracks Publishing, 2010.

Further Readings

Golf Magazine. *The Best Short Game Instruction Book Ever!* New York: Time Inc. Home Entertainment, 2009.

Hogan, Ben, with Herbert Warren Wind. *Five Lessons: The Modern Fundamentals of Golf*. New York: Simon & Schuster, 1957.

Penick, Harvey, with Bud Shrake. *Harvey Penick's Little Red Book*. New York: Simon & Schuster, 1992.

Simmons, Richard. *The Young Golfer: A Young Enthusiast's Guide to Golf*. New York: DK Publishing, 1999.

Werner, Doug. *Golfer's Start-Up: A Beginner's Guide to Golf*. San Diego: Tracks Publishing, 2010.

Web Links

To learn more about golf, visit ABDO Publishing Company online at **www.abdopublishing.com**. Web sites about golf are featured on our Book Links page. These links are routinely monitored and updated to provide the most current information available.

Places to Visit

USGA Museum
77 Liberty Corner Road
Far Hills, NJ 07931
(908) 234-2300 ext. 1057
www.usgamuseum.com/visit_museum

The museum has a large collection of golf memorabilia and artifacts showcasing the greatest champions and moments in US golf history. The USGA Library, located in the Arnold Palmer Center for Golf History, boasts the world's largest comprehensive golf literature and research collections. There is also a putting green.

World Golf Hall of Fame
World Golf Village
1 World Golf Place
St. Augustine, FL 32092
(904) 940-4123
www.worldgolfhalloffame.org

This hall of fame includes exhibits and memorabilia about the history of golf. Tickets to the museum include one shot on the Challenge Hole and a round on the 18-hole putting course. It is located in World Golf Village, a resort with hotel accommodations, championship golf courses, and the PGA Tour Golf Academy.

Index

bunker, 14, 30–33, 35

Carner, JoAnne, 22
clubs, 6, 11, 24, 33, 35, 38, 41, 43

Daniel, Beth, 14
driving, 4, 6–11, 24, 28, 35
    positioning, 9–11
    Quick Tip, 11
    speed, 10–11
    swing, 9–11

fairway, 4, 9, 14, 36, 40, 42

Gilchrist, Gary (coach), 17

Jutanugarn, Ariya, 23

Kerr, Cristie, 4, 8
Ko, Lydia, 11, 20, 22–24, 26–27, 30, 35

Ladies Professional Golf Association
    (LPGA), 6, 12, 22, 36, 39, 40
Lee, Bo-Mee, 14
Lewis, Stacy, 12, 14, 16–19, 22
Lincicome, Brittany, 4, 6–11, 19

Marriott, Lynn (coach), 40
McPherson, Kristy, 4, 6, 8
mental game, 12, 14, 16–19
    pressure, 12, 14, 16, 18–19
    Quick Tip, 19
    visualization, 16–17

Niethe, David (coach), 27
Nilsson, Pia (coach), 40
Nirapathpongporn, Virada, 31

Park, Inbee, 12, 16, 22
putting, 20, 22–27
    alignment, 24
    distance control, 25
    grip, 24, 25, 27
    Quick Tip, 27
    smooth stroke, 24

short game, 28, 30–33, 35
    clubs, 33, 35
    distance control, 32–33
    Quick Tip, 35
    shots, 33
    swing, 33
Sorenstam, Annika, 36, 38–43

Thompson, Lexi, 17
total game, 36, 38–43
    focus, 40–41
    pre-shot routine, 41–42, 43
    Quick Tip, 43
Tseng, Yani, 17–18, 28, 30–31

US Women's Amateur Championship
    2012, 22, 23, 30

Wie, Michelle, 28, 30–31
Wilson, Guy (coach), 22, 27

ABOUT THE AUTHOR

Maryann Hudson is a former award-winning sportswriter for the *Los Angeles Times*. She is a graduate of the University of Southern California's School of Journalism. She currently is a freelance writer and lives with her family in Pasadena, California.